Contents

Introduction

Holmes looked at her carefully. 'Is typing difficult when you have weak eyes?' he asked her.

'It was when I started,' she answered. 'But now I don't have to look down at my fingers, and – oh! How did you know?'

Holmes laughed. 'I'm a detective,' he said. 'It's my job.'

Sherlock Holmes is a very clever man. He sees the little things. He finds answers to some of the strangest and most difficult problems when other detectives – and his friend Dr Watson – cannot begin to understand them.

This happens in each of the three stories in this book.

Why did a man *type* his name at the end of a letter? Why did somebody sit in *that* chair when there were other chairs in the room? Why does a man follow a young woman on his bicycle, but never talk to her? These are important questions for Sherlock Holmes.

People read Sherlock Holmes stories and books in many different languages. They also watch the detective in films and on television. In one of the stories, Holmes died. The writer, Sir Arthur Conan Doyle, had to bring him back to life again, because people wanted to read more about the great detective.

Arthur Conan Doyle was born in Edinburgh, in Scotland, in 1859 and died in 1930. He was a doctor, but then he began writing. Between 1887 and 1927 he wrote sixty stories about Sherlock Holmes. *Sherlock Holmes and the Mystery of Boscombe Pool, A Scandal in Bohemia, The Return of Sherlock Holmes, Three Adventures of Sherlock Homes, The Hound of the Baskervilles* and *Sherlock Holmes Short Stories* are all Penguin Readers.

Sherlock Holmes and the Strange Mr Angel

Sherlock Holmes looked down from his flat into the London street.

'Ah, Watson! Somebody is coming here,' he said. 'Look, there, across the street!'

I went to the window and saw a large woman in a big hat. She looked up at us.

'*Is* she coming?' I said. 'Look, she isn't moving.'

'It's difficult for her,' Holmes answered. 'She wants help, but – ah, she's coming now.'

The woman walked slowly across Baker Street to Holmes's front door.

'She has a problem,' Holmes said.

'A problem?'

'It's a man,' Holmes said. 'She doesn't understand him, so she wants my help.'

Some minutes later, Miss Mary Sutherland came into Holmes's room. She told us her name and sat down in a chair.

Holmes looked at her carefully.

'Is typing difficult when you have weak eyes?' he asked her.

'It was when I started,' she answered. 'But now I don't have to look down at my fingers, and – oh! How did you know?'

Holmes laughed. 'I'm a detective,' he said. 'It's my job. This is my friend, Dr Watson. Now, tell me, why do you want to see me?'

'I want you to find somebody for me,' Miss Sutherland said. 'His name is Mr Hosmer Angel. I'm not rich, but I can pay you. I have one hundred pounds a year and the money from my typing. My father – Mr Windibank – doesn't know that I'm here. He doesn't want help from you or from the police. He says that I have to forget Mr Angel. But I can't do that.'

'Your father?' Holmes said. 'Your names are different.'

'I call him my father,' she said. 'It's strange, because he's only five years older than me. My mother married him a short time after my father died. He's nearly fifteen years younger than her. He works for a wine company.'

'Where does your hundred pounds a year come from?' Holmes asked.

I looked at Holmes.

'Why is he interested in that?' I thought. 'She wants to talk about Mr Angel, not her money.'

'The money came from my Uncle Ned in New Zealand, after he died,' Miss Sutherland said.

'That's very interesting,' Holmes said. 'So you have one hundred pounds a year, and the money from your typing job. Where does the money go?'

'I'm living at home, so I give my mother and father the hundred pounds,' she answered. 'Mr Windibank gets it from my bank and gives it to my mother. *I* use the money from my typing work.'

'Thank you for telling me that,' Holmes said. 'Now, tell us about you and Mr Hosmer Angel.'

Miss Sutherland's face went red and she looked down at her hands.

'I first met him at a dance,' she said.

'A dance?'

'Yes. Every year before he died, my father had tickets for a dance. Now my mother gets the tickets. Mr Windibank didn't want us to go to the dance. "They're not very nice people," he said. "And you haven't got the right clothes." But then he went to France.'

'What did he do in France?'

'He buys wine there,' Miss Sutherland answered. 'He often goes for two or three days. So my mother and I went to the dance.'

'Was Mr Windibank angry when he heard about that?' Holmes asked.

'No, he was very nice about it. He laughed and said, "You can't stop women when they really want to do something."'

'And you met Mr Hosmer Angel at the dance.'

'Yes, I met him that night,' Miss Sutherland said.

'When did you see him again?'

'He came to the house the next day. After that, I went for walks with him. But then Father came back from France, and Hosmer couldn't come to the house.'

'No?'

'No. Father doesn't like it when I have visitors,' Miss Sutherland said sadly.

'What did Mr Angel do next?' Holmes asked.

'He wrote me a letter every day,' Miss Sutherland answered. 'Then, a week later, Father went to France again and Hosmer visited me.'

'Did Mr Angel want to marry you?'

'Oh, yes, Mr Holmes,' Miss Sutherland said.

'When did he ask you?'

'He asked me after that first walk. He worked in an office in Leadenhall Street and –'

'Which office?' Holmes asked quickly.

'I don't know.'

'Where did he live?'

'In a room above the office,' she answered. 'I don't know the address. Only Leadenhall Street.'

'So where did you send your letters?'

'To the Leadenhall Street Post Office,' she told him. 'Hosmer went there for them. They were a secret from the other men in the office.'

'Why?' Holmes asked.

'He said, "I don't want them to know about you. They'll laugh at me." I said, "I can type the letters. Then they won't know about us." But he didn't want me to type them.'

'Tell me about him,' Holmes said.

'He was a very quiet man, a kind man. He liked to walk with me in the evening when there weren't many people on the street.'

'And his clothes?'

'He had nice clothes,' she said. 'He wore dark glasses because he had weak eyes. He spoke quietly, too.'

'What happened after Mr Windibank went back to France?' Holmes asked.

'Mr Hosmer Angel came to the house again,' Miss Sutherland said. 'He met my mother. Then one day he said, "Strange things happen in this life. But I want to know that you will always love me." He wanted to marry me on the Friday of that week.'

'What did your mother say?'

'My mother was happy about that because she liked him, too,' Miss Sutherland said. 'I said, "But aren't we going to ask Father?" She said, "No, we can tell him later." But I didn't want to do that. So I wrote to Father in Bordeaux.'

'Bordeaux?'

'Yes. The company has its French office there. But the letter came back to me on the Friday morning.'

'It was too late?' Holmes said.

'Yes. He left for England before it arrived.'

'What happened on that Friday?'

'Hosmer came in a cab to our house,' Miss Sutherland said. 'The cab took Mother and me to the church, near King's Cross. Hosmer followed us in a different cab. Mother and I arrived at the church first. When the other cab arrived, we waited. But Hosmer didn't get out. There was nobody in the cab. "What happened to him?" the cab driver said. "He got *in*. I saw him." That was last Friday, Mr Holmes. Where is Hosmer?

4

'What happened to him?' the cab driver said. 'He got in.'

What's he doing? Why can't he write me a letter? Oh, I'm so unhappy!'

Holmes thought about her story.

'That was very unkind,' he said.

'Oh, but he's *kind*, Mr Holmes. That morning he said to me again, "Strange things happen, but I'll always love you. I *will* marry you." Now I understand. He was afraid of something. And he was right! Something bad happened to him – I know it!'

'But what?' Holmes asked.

'I don't know,' Miss Sutherland said sadly.

'Was your mother angry?'

'Yes. She doesn't want to hear Hosmer's name again.'

'And you told Mr Windibank about it?'

'Yes,' she answered. 'Father doesn't understand it. He wants me to forget about Hosmer. But he thinks that he'll come back to me. Why does a man leave a woman at the doors of the church, Mr Holmes? Hosmer didn't have my money. He never asked me for money. He really wanted to marry me. But where is he now? And why can't he write to me? I think about it day and night, Mr Holmes. I can't sleep.'

Miss Sutherland began to cry.

'I'll find the answers to your questions,' Holmes said. 'But please forget Mr Hosmer Angel.'

'Will I see him again?' she asked.

'I'm sorry – no, you won't. Have you got his letters? Can you give them to me?'

'Here are four of them,' Miss Sutherland said. 'And here's an advertisement. I put it in last Saturday's newspaper.'

'Thank you. What's your address?'

'31 Lyon Place, Camberwell,' she told him.

'And what's the name of Mr Windibank's company?' Holmes asked.

'He works for Westhouse and Marbank, the wine company.'

'Thank you,' Holmes said. 'Now forget about this man. Think about your future.'

'You're very kind, Mr Holmes, but I can't do that,' she said. 'I'll always love Hosmer. I'll be there when he comes back. I'll wait for him.'

After she left, Sherlock Holmes sat quietly for some minutes.

'An interesting young woman,' he said.

'The typing,' I said. 'How did you know?'

'Her arms, above her hands,' Holmes said. 'There were red lines across them. A typist puts her arms on the front of her desk when she types. That leaves a line. There was also a line across her nose. She wears glasses –'

'For her weak eyes. Of course!'

'These things aren't difficult, Watson.'

'They aren't difficult for *you*, Holmes,' I said.

'Now, read the advertisement,' he said. 'What does it say about Mr Angel's clothes, hair and face?'

I read some of it to him:

'... *a big man with black hair, a black beard and dark glasses ... speaks quietly ... wore a black coat, grey trousers ... worked in an office in Leadenhall Street ...*'

Holmes looked at the letters from Hosmer Angel to Miss Sutherland.

'These tell us nothing about Mr Angel,' he said. 'But there's one strange thing.'

'He typed them,' I said.

'Yes. Not only the letters, but also his name,' Holmes said. 'And there's no address, only Leadenhall Street. But the name is important.'

'Is it?'

'Of course, Watson. Now, I'll write two letters. One letter to a company, and the other letter to Mr Windibank.'

'To Windibank?'

'Yes. I'll invite him to this flat at six o'clock tomorrow evening. Before that, I hope we'll have some answers.'

♦

When I arrived at his flat at six o'clock the next evening, Sherlock Holmes was half asleep in his chair.

'Do you have the answers?' I asked him.

'To the letters?'

'To them, yes, and to Miss Sutherland's problem,' I said. 'Who was the man, and why did he leave her at the church? And will she see him again?'

But before Holmes could tell me, Mr Windibank arrived. He was a big man with grey eyes, about thirty years old. He sat down in the nearest chair.

'Good evening, Mr Windibank,' Holmes said.

'Good evening, Mr Holmes,' Mr Windibank said.

'I've got your note here,' Holmes said. ' "I will be with you at six o'clock. James Windibank." Did *you* type this?'

'Yes. I'm a little late,' Mr Windibank said. 'I'm sorry. I'm sorry, too, about Miss Sutherland. I didn't want her to come here. This is a family problem and you can't help —'

'Oh, but I can,' Holmes said.

Mr Windibank looked at him.

'You — you can?' he said. 'That's — that's wonderful.'

'It's strange,' Holmes said. 'All typewriters are different after people use them for some time.'

'Are they?' Mr Windibank said.

'Yes. Look at your note, Mr Windibank. The letter *e* is darker than the other letters. And the bottom of the letter *r* isn't there. Do you see? There are fourteen other little things, but you can see these two easily.'

'We use this typewriter for our letters at the office,' our visitor said. 'It's quite old now.'

'And here are the four letters from Mr Angel,' Holmes said. 'He typed every letter. In each of them, the letter *e* is darker than the other letters. And you can't see the bottom of the *r*.'

Mr Windibank jumped out of his chair.

'I'm a busy man,' he said angrily. 'I can't sit here and listen to this stupid talk. When you catch the man, tell me.'

'All right, I will,' Holmes said. He went to the door and locked it. 'I'll tell you now. I caught him!'

'What! Where?' Mr Windibank shouted.

'Sit down and listen, Mr Windibank. This wasn't a difficult problem.'

Our visitor fell back into the chair. His face was white.

'The – the police can do nothing to me!' he said.

'You're right. But I'm sorry about that,' Holmes said. 'A young woman is in love with a cold, unkind man. Now listen to my story . . . A man married an older woman for her money, and for her daughter's money. The daughter's money was important to the woman, and to her husband. They didn't want to lose one hundred pounds a year when she got married. They didn't want her to leave home. So, what could this man do? He didn't want her to have friends of her age, so people couldn't come to the house. She couldn't go out to dances. And then he and his wife made a plan.'

'We didn't want to *hurt* her,' Mr Windibank said. 'We – we didn't think –'

'No!' Holmes said. 'You didn't think about the feelings of a young woman in love. But she *did* love him. They went for walks. He was kind to her. Her mother told her, "He's a nice man." The man asked the young woman, "Will you marry me?" and the young woman said yes.

'But, of course, he couldn't really marry her. He had a wife – the young woman's mother. It had to end. But he didn't want her to marry another nice young man. So he said to her, "Will you wait for me?" And because she loved him, she said yes. And Mr James Windibank is happy because, for years and years, Miss Sutherland will wait for Mr Hosmer Angel. She won't marry another man.

'Mr Angel sent the young woman to the church door with her mother in the first cab. Then he climbed into the next cab, through one door – *and out of the other door!* He didn't go to the church! Am I right, Mr Windibank?'

'Perhaps you are,' said our visitor. 'Perhaps you aren't.' He got up from his chair and looked at Holmes with cold eyes. 'But you can't lock the door. I don't have to stay here. The police will – '

'Oh, the police can do nothing to you!' Holmes said angrily. 'I know that.' He unlocked the door. 'But does the young woman have a brother or a friend? I hope she does. And I hope he hurts you and – ! No, I won't wait for that. *I'll* do it!'

Mr Windibank ran through the door before Holmes could catch him. A minute later, we looked out of the window and saw him running very fast down the road.

'One day that man will do something very, very bad,' Holmes said. 'And the police *will* catch him.'

'I hope you're right, Holmes,' I said.

Holmes sat down in his chair.

'But it was an interesting problem, Watson.'

'How did you know –?' I began.

'Mr Hosmer Angel was a strange man,' Holmes said. 'But what did he want? I thought about Miss Sutherland's family. Who did well from all this? Her mother – and Mr James Windibank. Miss Sutherland stayed at home, so her money didn't leave their house. And the two men – Angel and Windibank – were never in the same place at the same time. Angel only visited the house when Mr Windibank was away.'

'That's right!' I said.

'That was strange,' Holmes said. 'The dark glasses and the

Mr Windibank ran through the door before Holmes could catch him.

beard were also very strange. And why did Mr Angel *type* his name? Because Miss Sutherland knew her father's writing!'

'Who did you write the other letter to?' I asked.

'Mr Windibank worked for Westhouse and Marbank,' Holmes said. 'I wrote to them.'

'What did you say?'

'I asked them about the man in the advertisement – but *without* the glasses and the beard. I also, of course, wrote to Mr Windibank and invited him here. I had Mr Angel's letters to Miss Sutherland, and Mr Windibank typed his note on the same typewriter. The letter from Westhouse and Marbank gave me James Windibank's name. After that, it was easy.'

'Will you tell Miss Sutherland all this?' I asked.

'No,' Holmes said. 'She's a woman. She'll always think kindly of Mr Hosmer Angel, and I can't stop her.'

Sherlock Holmes and the Important Exam Paper

Sherlock Holmes and I went on a visit to one of our great university cities.

'Perhaps somebody here will have a problem, Holmes,' I said, 'and come to you for help.'

'I'm going to be busy with other work, Watson,' Holmes said. 'I want to look at some books at the university. I don't want other people's problems.'

But somebody *did* want help.

Hilton Soames, a teacher at the university, came to see us. He was a tall, thin man and was very excited about something.

'Can you give me an hour or two of your time, Mr Holmes?' he asked. 'Something happened this afternoon.'

'I'm very busy,' Holmes said. 'Perhaps the police can help you. Why don't you ask them?'

'No, no, not the police,' Mr Soames said. 'We don't want strangers to know about this problem. You're the right person, Mr Holmes. Only you can help.'

'All right,' Holmes said. 'Tell me. What happened?'

'Tomorrow is the first day of some important exams,' Mr Soames said. 'The exam papers are, of course, secret. Every student would like to see them before the exam, so we are very careful with them.

'I teach Greek, and at three o'clock today the Greek exam paper arrived in my office. I had to read it carefully for the last time, because there can be no mistakes. But at four-thirty I went out to a friend's house for tea. I left the exam paper – three pages – on my desk, but I locked my door.'

'How long were you out?' Holmes asked.

'For about an hour,' Mr Soames answered. 'When I came back, there was a key in my door! It wasn't my key. I had my key in my coat.'

'Does your servant have a key?'

'Yes,' Mr Soames said. 'Bannister is a good man, Mr Holmes, but it *was* his key. He visited my room five or ten minutes after I left it.'

'Why?' Holmes asked.

'He brings me tea every afternoon. Today he forgot about the visit to my friend.'

'And he left his key in your door when he went out,' Holmes said.

'Yes. He's usually very careful, but −'

'But not today,' Holmes said.

'No, not today,' Mr Soames said.

'So you went into your room −'

'Yes, and the exam paper was there, but only one page was on the desk.'

'Where were the other two pages?'

'One was on the table near the window. The other page was on the floor.'

Holmes was suddenly interested.

'The first page was on the floor,' he said slowly. 'The second page was on the table near the window. And the third page was on your desk. Am I right?'

'Yes, that's right!' Mr Soames said. 'How do you know that?'

'Finish your very interesting story,' Holmes told him.

'I called Bannister,' Mr Soames said. 'He felt ill when I told him about the exam paper. I asked him, "Did you look at my papers?" He said no, and he *is* a good man, Mr Holmes. I gave him a glass of wine and he sat down. Next, I looked carefully round the room.'

'Did you find anything?' Holmes asked.

'Yes!' Mr Soames said. 'Somebody broke a pencil near the table by the window.'

'How do you know?'

'There were small pieces of wood from a pencil on the table,' Mr Soames said. 'And that's not all. There was a very small piece of black clay on the table, too.'

'That's interesting,' Holmes said.

'One more thing,' Mr Soames said. 'I have a new desk – but now there's a cut on it!'

Holmes thought for a minute or two, then he said, 'I'll help you, Mr Soames. Now, tell me something. Did anybody visit you in your room after the exam paper came to you?'

'Yes, young Daulat Ras, an Indian student,' Mr Soames said. 'He wanted to ask me about the exam. But he couldn't read the paper. I put a book on top of it.'

'But he saw it,' Holmes said. 'He saw the exam paper on your desk before you hid it?'

'Perhaps.'

'Did any other people know about the exam paper? Did Bannister?'

'No,' Mr Soames said. 'Nobody.'

'Where is Bannister now?'

'I left him in my room.'

'Did you leave your door open?' Holmes asked.

'Yes, but I locked the paper in my desk first,' Mr Soames said.

'Let's go to your office,' Holmes said.

Mr Soames's office was on the ground floor of an old building. Above it were three students' rooms.

From outside, Holmes looked through a window into Mr Soames's office.

'This window doesn't open,' Mr Soames said. 'Nobody can get in here.'

'I can see that,' Holmes said.

After a minute, we went inside. Mr Soames unlocked his door and we went into his room.

Holmes stood by the door and looked carefully at the floor.

Then he said, 'Your servant isn't here now. Perhaps he's feeling better. Which chair did he sit on?'

'The chair by the window.'

15

'Near that little table?' Holmes went across the room and looked at it. 'So ... the man came in and took the paper from your desk. He carried it to the table by the window. Why? He wanted to see you when you came from your friend's room.'

'But he couldn't see me,' Mr Soames said. 'I came in through the back door.'

'Ah, that's good!' Holmes said. 'But that was his plan. Now, let's look at the three pages.'

Mr Soames took them out of his desk and gave them to Holmes. The detective looked at them carefully.

'He carried this page across the room first and looked at it,' Holmes said. 'Then he wrote down the exam questions. Fifteen minutes? Perhaps. Then he threw the first page on the floor and took the second page. He started to write down those questions, but then he heard you at the back door. He couldn't put the papers back on your desk – there was no time. So he ran out of the room. Did you hear him on the stairs?'

'No,' Mr Soames said.

'He wrote quickly and he broke his pencil,' Holmes said. 'Look at these pieces, Watson. It was a dark blue pencil. This piece has the letters *NN* on it. What does that mean? Is it the end of a word? *Johann*, perhaps? There are Johann Faber pencils.'

'Yes, that's right!' I said.

Holmes went to the desk.

'Is this the piece of black clay?'

He took it in his fingers. It was small and round.

'Yes,' Mr Soames said.

Holmes looked carefully at the small cut on the top of the desk.

'This is very interesting,' he said. 'A line, and then a cut.' He looked at a door across the room. 'Where does that go?'

'To my bedroom,' Mr Soames answered.

'Look at these pieces, Watson.'

'Did you go in there before you came for me?'

'No, I didn't.'

Holmes walked across the room to the door and looked into the bedroom.

'A nice room!' he said. 'Please wait outside. I'm going to look at the floor.' He did this carefully, then said, 'No, I can't see anything. What's this cupboard? Oh, for your clothes. But wait! What's this on the cupboard floor? It's more black clay! So your visitor came into your bedroom, Mr Soames.'

'But why?' Mr Soames asked. 'Why did he come in here?'

'He hid here!' Holmes said. 'He heard you at the back door. Then he ran in here and hid in this cupboard.'

'So he was in the cupboard when Bannister and I were in the next room!'

'Yes, he was. How many students live upstairs? Three, did you say? And they all go past your door.'

'Yes,' Mr Soames said.

'Who are they?'

'There's Gilchrist,' Mr Soames told him. 'He's a nice, strong young man. He's very good at games and he likes running. His father was Sir Jabez Gilchrist.'

'Sir Jabez Gilchrist?' Holmes said. 'What do I know about him? Oh, yes. He was a very rich man, but not very clever. He lost his money – every penny.'

'That's right. Young Gilchrist has little money, but he works hard. Daulat Ras lives above Gilchrist. He's a quiet young man, but he's a good student. Miles McLaren lives above him. He's very clever, but he doesn't like working. The exam won't be easy for him.'

'That's interesting,' Holmes said. 'Now, let's talk to your servant, Bannister.'

Mr Soames called Bannister into the office. He was a small man, about fifty years old. His face was grey; he didn't look well.

He played with his fingers unhappily when he answered Holmes's questions.

'You left your key in the door, Bannister?' Holmes asked.

'Yes, sir,' the servant told him. 'I don't usually leave it.'

'When did you come into this room?'

'At about half-past four. It's Mr Soames's tea time. But he wasn't here, so I went away.'

'Did you look at the papers on his desk?' Holmes asked.

'No, sir, I did not!' Bannister answered quickly.

'But you left your key in the door.'

'I had the tea in my hands,' Bannister said. 'I forgot about the key. I felt very bad about it later, sir. It made me ill.'

'Where were you when you began to feel ill?'

'Here, near the door.'

'But you sat down in *that* chair – there,' Holmes said. 'Why did you walk past the other chairs?'

'I don't know, sir,' Bannister said.

'Of course he doesn't remember, Mr Holmes,' Mr Soames said. 'He was quite ill at that time.'

'Mr Soames left you here because he wanted to find me,' Holmes said to Bannister. 'How long did you stay after Mr Soames went out?'

'Two or three minutes,' Bannister answered. 'Then I locked the door and went to my room.'

'That's all, Bannister, thank you,' Holmes said. 'Mr Soames, can we go for a walk outside?'

We went out into the garden. It was nearly dark now. We looked up at the outside of the house. There were lights on in the three rooms above Mr Soames's office.

'Your three students are all in their rooms,' Holmes said to Mr Soames. 'One of them isn't a happy man.'

We could see the Indian student, Daulat Ras. He walked up and down his room.

'I'd like to visit each of them,' Holmes said. 'Is that possible?'

'Yes, of course,' Mr Soames said. 'People often visit these rooms. The building is old and very interesting.'

We went first to Gilchrist's door.

'No names, please!' Holmes told Mr Soames.

After a minute, a tall young man opened the door.

'These visitors would like to see your room, Gilchrist,' Mr Soames said. 'They're interested in old buildings.'

'Please, come in,' Gilchrist said.

He showed us round his room. Holmes was very interested.

'A beautiful room,' he said.

He started to write notes about it in his notebook, but his pencil broke.

'Oh, dear,' Holmes said.

'Use my pencil,' Gilchrist said.

'Thank you.'

Holmes looked carefully at Gilchrist's pencil.

Strangely, the same accident happened in Daulat Ras's room.

'A very interesting room,' Holmes said, and started writing in his notebook. Then he broke his pencil.

'Oh, dear,' he said.

'Use one of my pencils,' Ras said.

'Thank you.'

Holmes looked carefully at Daulat Ras's pencil.

Miles McLaren didn't open his door.

'Can we come in, McLaren?' Mr Soames shouted. 'These visitors would like to see your room.'

'Go away!' McLaren shouted from behind the door. 'I've got an exam tomorrow, and I'm busy. I can't see anybody!'

'I'm sorry,' Mr Soames said to us. 'He's not an easy student.'

'How tall is he?' Holmes asked.

'How tall? He's taller than Daulat Ras, but not as tall as Gilchrist.'

'That's quite important. And now, Mr Soames, thank you and good night.'

'Oh, are you going, Mr Holmes?' Mr Soames cried. 'But tomorrow is the exam! What am I going to do about it? I can't –'

'I'll come here early tomorrow morning,' Holmes told him. 'I'll have answers for you then.'

'But –' Mr Soames began.

'Everything will be all right,' Holmes said. 'I'll take the black clay and the pieces of pencil with me. Goodbye.'

When we were outside, Holmes looked at me.

'It's an interesting little problem,' he said. 'Three young men. But which young man went into Mr Soames's room and began to write down the questions from the exam paper? Which student was it, Watson?'

'McLaren, the student in the top room,' I said.

'Why?'

'He does no work and the exam will be difficult for him. Or perhaps it's the Indian student. Why did he walk up and down in his room? Is he afraid of something?'

'A lot of people walk up and down when they're learning something,' Holmes said. 'And the pencils don't help us. But one man *is* interesting.'

'Who?'

'Bannister, the servant.'

'But Mr Soames says that he's a good man.'

'Yes,' Holmes said. 'So why did –? Ah, here's the first shop, Watson.'

'Shop?'

I looked round. We were outside a small shop. It sold pens, pencils, paper and envelopes.

'We'll begin asking questions here,' Holmes said.

There were four of these shops in the town and we went to all of them. On each visit, Holmes showed the man in the shop the pieces of pencil.

'Do you know this pencil?' he asked them.

Each man told him, 'We haven't got any, but we can get them for you.'

Holmes was not unhappy about this.

'It's getting late, Watson,' he said. 'Let's have dinner.'

We didn't talk about the three students again that night, and Holmes was very quiet. After dinner, I watched him for a time. Then I went to bed.

♦

Holmes came to my room at eight o'clock the next morning.

'Do you have any answers?' I asked him.

'Yes, Watson, I have,' he said. 'I got up very early this morning. I found *this* five kilometres away!'

He showed me his hand. In it were three little pieces of black clay.

'Holmes, you only had two yesterday,' I said.

'And where did all three come from?' he said. 'The same place! Now, let's go and see Mr Soames.'

Mr Soames was in his room. He looked very unhappy.

'What can I do, Mr Holmes? Will there be an exam?'

'Yes, Mr Soames,' Holmes said. 'There will be an exam today.'

'But the young man – ?'

'He won't take it.'

'You know him?' Mr Soames said.

'Yes. Call Bannister.'

'Bannister?' Mr Soames said. 'Oh, all right.'

Bannister came into the room a minute or two later.

'Please close the door,' Holmes said. 'Now, tell me – what *really* happened yesterday?'

Bannister's face went white. 'I – I told you everything, sir,' he said.

'Did you? There's nothing more?'

'No, sir.'

'Then *I'll* tell *you*,' Holmes said. 'When you sat down on that chair yesterday, you hid something.'

'No, sir!' Bannister said.

'Yes. There was a young man in Mr Soames's bedroom cupboard. You knew that then. When Mr Soames left the room, you called him. The young man came out.'

Bannister suddenly looked afraid.

'There was no young man, sir,' he said.

'All right,' Holmes said. 'Go and stand near the bedroom door.' He turned to Mr Soames. 'Mr Soames, please go and find young Gilchrist.'

Holmes, Bannister and I waited. Minutes later, Mr Soames came back with the student. Gilchrist was a tall, strong young man with blue eyes.

'Mr Gilchrist,' Holmes said, 'why did you come into Mr Soames's room yesterday?'

Gilchrist looked at us, then at Bannister.

'No, Mr Gilchrist!' Bannister said quickly. 'I said nothing! Not one word!'

'No, but you're talking now,' Holmes said. 'Gilchrist, tell us! It's not a secret now.'

Gilchrist put his head in his hands and began to cry.

Holmes went across the room and put an arm round him.

'It's all right,' he said kindly. 'You made a mistake, but you're sorry now. I know that. I'll tell Mr Soames the story. You can tell me when I'm wrong.' He turned to Mr Soames. 'My first question was, "How did the student know about the exam paper?" It was here on your desk, but how did he know that? I looked at your window from the outside, Mr Soames. Do you remember?'

'I remember,' Mr Soames said. 'But nobody can get in through that window.'

'When I looked through the window, I could see the papers on your desk,' Holmes said. 'I'm a tall man. A shorter man couldn't see them. So, I looked for a tall man. And the black clay and the cut on your desk? I didn't understand them. Then I remembered something – Gilchrist likes running. There's clay out on the running ground. I know that because I found some there this morning. And running shoes have spikes on the bottom of them.'

'Yes!' I said.

'Gilchrist went past your window, Mr Soames,' Holmes told him. 'He looked inside. Because he's tall, he could see the papers. Were they exam papers? He didn't know. Then he went past your door and saw the key – Bannister's key. Suddenly, he had to see those papers! He had to know. He came into the room and – yes! – there was the Greek exam paper! Gilchrist put his running shoes on the desk –'

'And cut the desk with the spikes!' I cried.

'Yes, Watson,' Holmes said. He turned to Gilchrist again. 'What did you put on the chair near the window?'

'My – my notebook,' Gilchrist said.

'You put your notebook on the chair,' Holmes said. 'Then you began to look at the first two pages of the exam paper. You watched for Mr Soames, but he came through the back door. What did you do? You took your running shoes from the desk. Then you ran into the bedroom and hid in the cupboard. *But you forgot your notebook.* Also, a piece of the clay from your shoes fell on to the desk. More fell in the cupboard.' Holmes looked hard at the student. 'Am I right, Mr Gilchrist?'

'Yes,' Gilchrist said. He looked at the floor. 'Yes, you're right. I'm very sorry. I made a mistake.'

'Is that all?' Mr Soames asked angrily.

'No, sir,' Gilchrist said. 'I have a letter here, Mr Soames. I wrote it to you early this morning. It says that I'm not going to take the

'Because he's tall, he could see the papers.'

exam. I'm going to work for the South African police. They want me to work for them, and I'm leaving today.'

'Good,' Mr Soames said. 'You can't take the exam now.'

'Mr Bannister told me that, too,' Gilchrist said.

Holmes turned and looked at the servant.

'Bannister, why did you help Gilchrist?' he asked. 'You hid his notebook. You called to him after Mr Soames left his room. Why?'

'I worked for Mr Gilchrist's father,' Bannister answered, 'before he lost all his money.'

'Sir Jabez Gilchrist,' Holmes said.

'Yes,' Bannister said. 'Sir Jabez was always good to me. When he lost his money, I found work here at the university.'

'And you watched his son. You helped him when you could,' Holmes said.

'Yes, Mr Holmes. Yesterday, I saw the notebook on the chair and I thought, "That's Mr Gilchrist's notebook!" I quickly understood about the exam paper. Yes, I sat on the notebook and hid it. Yes, I called Mr Gilchrist after Mr Soames left the room. Mr Gilchrist told me everything. I listened, then I said to him, "You're a fine young man, Mr Gilchrist. You know that you can't take the exam now." He understood that. I had to help him, Mr Holmes. Was I wrong?'

'No. He listened to you – and everybody makes mistakes.'

Holmes turned to Mr Soames.

'Mr Soames, you have the answer to your little problem.' He looked at the student. 'And I hope you do well in South Africa, Gilchrist. Come, Watson. It's time for breakfast!'

Sherlock Holmes and the Dangerous Road

Miss Violet Smith came to Sherlock Holmes's flat in Baker Street late one Saturday evening. She was a beautiful young woman.

'*Please* help me, Mr Holmes,' she said.

Holmes gave a tired smile. He had other problems at that time.

'Sit down, Miss Smith,' he said. 'You don't have the grey face of a city person. You live in the country?'

'Yes, near Farnham, in Surrey,' she said, and she began to tell us her story. 'My father is dead, Mr Holmes, but he had a brother. My uncle, Ralph Smith, lived in South Africa. After my father died, my mother and I didn't have much money. Then, one day, we saw an advertisement in *The Times* newspaper. Somebody wanted us to go to an address in London. Mother and I went there, and we met two men – Mr Carruthers and Mr Woodley. They were in England on a visit from South Africa.

'Uncle Ralph was their friend, but he was dead. Before he died, he asked for their help. He wanted Mr Carruthers and Mr Woodley to find my mother and me. It was very strange. For years my uncle never wrote to us or looked for us. Why was he suddenly interested in us at the end? Mr Carruthers said, "He heard about your father, and he wanted to help you."'

'When did you see these two men?' Holmes asked.

'Last December,' she answered. 'I didn't like Mr Woodley. He was . . . *too* friendly. Do you understand?'

'Yes, I understand,' Holmes said. 'He was . . . interested in you?'

Miss Smith's face went very red.

'Yes, but I'm going to marry Cyril at the end of the summer. I'm not interested in other men. Mr Carruthers was older and nicer than Mr Woodley. He asked about money, and then he gave me some work. I didn't want to leave my mother, but Mr Carruthers wanted a music teacher for his young daughter. He said, "I'll pay you one hundred pounds a year, and you can go home to your mother every Saturday and Sunday."

'That's a lot of money for a music teacher, Mr Holmes. So I went down to Chiltern House and started to work for him. Mr Carruthers's wife is dead, but the child is lovely. Every Saturday, I go home for the weekend. At the beginning, everything went very well.

'Then Mr Woodley arrived. He stayed for a week, and he tried to kiss me. "I'm a rich man," he said. "Marry me and you can have everything." When I said no, he tried to kiss me again. Mr Carruthers came in and pulled him away. But Mr Woodley turned and hit Mr Carruthers in the face! That was the end of Mr Woodley's visits, of course. Mr Carruthers was very sorry. "It will never happen again," he told me.

'Every Saturday morning, Mr Holmes, I go to Farnham Station on my bicycle and I take the 12.22 train to London. The station is about ten kilometres from Chiltern House, and the road is very quiet. For about two kilometres it goes between a park and the trees in front of Charlington House. You don't usually meet anybody on that road, but one day I looked behind me. About two hundred metres away, there was a man on a bicycle. He was about forty or forty-five and had a short, dark beard. Before I got to Farnham, I looked behind me again. The man wasn't there.

'When I went back to Farnham on Monday, he was there again! The same man on the same road! And the next Saturday and Monday, it happened again. He didn't come near me or speak to me. But it was very strange. I told Mr Carruthers and he said, "I'll get a horse and trap. Then somebody can drive you to the station."

'The horse and trap didn't arrive this week, so I went to the station on my bicycle again this morning. And there was that man again! I don't know him, but he's always a long way away. I can't see his face, only his beard. He wears dark clothes and a hat.

'About two hundred metres away, there was a man on a bicycle.'

I wanted to know more about him, so I went slowly. He went slowly, too. Then I stopped – and *he* stopped. Next, I turned quickly at the end of the road and waited for him. But he didn't come. I went back and looked. He wasn't on the road. It was very strange.'

'Very interesting,' Holmes said. 'How long was it before you went back?'

'Two or three minutes,' she said.

'So he couldn't go back down the road,' Holmes said. 'He went into the park.'

'He didn't go into the park. I could see the park. There are no trees.'

'Perhaps he went to Charlington House.' Holmes didn't speak for a minute or two. Then he said, 'Where's your future husband?'

'Cyril? He's working in Coventry. The man on the bicycle is *not* Cyril, Mr Holmes.'

'And no other man is interested in you?' Holmes asked.

'I think that Mr Carruthers ... likes me,' she answered. 'A woman knows. But he doesn't say or do anything.'

'What's his job?' Holmes asked.

'He's a rich man,' Miss Smith said. 'He comes into London two or three times every week and visits company offices.'

'Thank you, Miss Smith,' Holmes said. 'I'm very busy, but I will think about your problem. Then I'll call you.'

After the front door closed, Holmes looked at me.

'Is the man on the bicycle a secret lover, Watson?' he said. 'Perhaps. But what's he doing on that road? It's strange.'

'He goes to the same place every time,' I said.

'Yes,' Holmes said. 'And there are other questions. Why did Carruthers *and* Woodley come from South Africa? Why does Carruthers pay one hundred pounds a year to a music teacher? And why doesn't he have a horse and trap when he lives ten kilometres from the station?'

'Will you go down there?'

'No, my friend,' he answered. '*You* will go down. I'm too busy. Go to Farnham on Monday. Arrive early, hide near the road and watch. Then ask about Charlington House. Who lives there?'

◆

Miss Smith always took the 9.50 train from London to Farnham. I went on an earlier train and quickly found the road from the station to Chiltern House.

I hid and waited. Then I saw a man on a bicycle. He wore a dark coat and trousers and he had a beard. It was him! I watched him carefully. He carried his bicycle into the trees.

Fifteen minutes later, Miss Smith arrived on her bicycle. The man with the beard came out from the trees and went after her. She looked back and saw him. She went slowly. He also went slowly. She stopped. He stopped. He was always about two hundred metres behind her. Suddenly, she turned her bicycle and went after him. But he was too quick for her. She turned back and went up the road again, to Chiltern House.

I waited. The man came slowly back on his bicycle and then went into the tall trees between the road and Charlington House. I ran across the road. I could see the house, but not the man.

In Farnham, I asked questions about Charlington House and learned the name of a London estate agency. On my way home, I went to the estate agency.

'An old man, Mr Williamson, is staying there for the summer,' a man told me. 'I can't tell you anything about him.'

That evening, Holmes listened to my story. He wasn't happy.

'Why did you hide in the park, Watson?' he said. 'You couldn't see the man from there. The man doesn't want Miss Smith to see his face. So I think she knows him. And then *you* didn't see his face. We also want to know his name, of course. So what did you do next, Watson? You went to a London estate agency!'

'What was wrong with that?' I asked.

'Why didn't you go to a bar in Charlington? The people of Charlington can tell you all about this man Williamson. The name tells me nothing. He's an old man, so he can't be the man on the bicycle. The man on the bicycle moves quickly when he wants to. Oh, don't look so sad, my friend. Perhaps *I* will ask some people questions.'

♦

The next morning, we had a note from Miss Smith. It ended:

I cannot stay here, Mr Holmes. Yesterday, Mr Carruthers asked me to marry him. Of course, I cannot do that: I am going to marry my Cyril. It is now very difficult for me at Chiltern House.

'This gets more and more interesting, Watson,' my friend said. 'I'll go down this afternoon.'

When he arrived back at Baker Street late that evening, he told me his story.

'I found a hotel and talked to some of the people in the bar,' he said.

'Could they tell you anything?' I asked.

'Of course,' Holmes said. 'One: Williamson is an old man with a white beard. Two: he was a vicar, but not now. Three: there are usually visitors to Charlington House on Saturdays and Sundays. Four: Mr Woodley is one of them.' Holmes smiled at me. 'I got these answers easily, Watson. But who came in from the next room of the hotel bar at that minute? *Woodley.* "Why are you interested in me?" he asked. "Who are you? What do you want?" Then he hit me! There was a short fight – and I won! Mr Woodley went home in a horse and trap! Me? I'm fine, Watson.'

The next letter from Miss Smith came on Thursday:

I am leaving my job with Mr Carruthers. On Saturday I will

'Who are you? What do you want?'

come up to London and I will not go back to Chiltern House. Mr Carruthers has a trap now, so the road to the station is not dangerous for me. But I cannot stay.

Mr Woodley came again. I did not meet him, but I saw him through a window. He has a big cut on his face – an accident, perhaps. He had a long talk with Mr Carruthers. Mr Carruthers was very excited after Mr Woodley left. Woodley did not sleep here, but I saw him again this morning in the garden. I am afraid of this man, but all will be well after Saturday.

'I hope she's right, Watson,' Holmes said. 'The two of us will go down on Saturday.'

◆

Holmes took his gun when we left on Saturday morning. It was a sunny day, a good day for a visit to the country. Holmes and I walked down the road and listened to the birds. We could see Charlington House.

'Look!' I cried. 'There's a horse and trap on the road.'

'Is that *her* trap?' Holmes said. 'Then she's going to catch an earlier train. She'll be past Charlington before we can meet her!'

Holmes began to run. He was a hundred metres away from me when he stopped. At the same time, I saw the horse and trap again. But now there was nobody in it.

'Stop the horse, Watson!' Holmes shouted. 'Oh, we're too late!'

I stopped the horse and we jumped into the trap. Holmes turned it round and we went back down the road.

'There! That's the man!' I shouted.

A man on a bicycle came up the road. It was the man with the beard. He looked up and saw us.

'Stop!' he shouted, and jumped from his bicycle. 'Where did you get that trap?'

He took a gun from his coat.

Holmes jumped down from the trap.

'Where is Miss Violet Smith?' he asked quickly.

'That's my question!' the man said. 'You're in her trap.'

'We met the trap on the road,' Holmes said. 'There was nobody in it.'

'Oh, no!' said the man. 'They've got her! Woodley and that vicar man. Are you her friends?'

'Yes!' I said.

'Then come with me!' he said.

He ran into the trees, and Holmes and I went after him.

'Wait!' Holmes said suddenly. 'Who is this?'

There was a young man on the ground.

'That's Peter,' said the man with the beard. 'He drives Mr Carruthers's trap.'

Peter began to move and open his eyes.

'He'll be all right. He can come after us in a minute,' said the man with the beard. 'Let's go!'

We ran through the trees. We stopped when we got to the garden outside the house. Suddenly, we heard a loud cry from a woman.

'This way! This way!' shouted the man with the beard.

We ran across the garden into open ground. There, under a tall tree, stood three people. One was Miss Violet Smith with her hands over her face. Opposite her stood a heavy man with a red face. It was Mr Woodley, and he was excited about something. Between them stood a short old man with a grey beard, in the clothes of a vicar. He turned and smiled at Mr Woodley.

'And now you are husband and wife,' he said.

'Quickly!' said our friend with the black beard.

He ran to the tall tree. Holmes and I went after him. Mr Williamson – the man in the vicar's clothes – saw us and smiled. Mr Woodley laughed when he saw the man with the beard.

'You can take off your beard, Bob,' he said. 'I know it's you. Say hello to my new wife!'

35

Our friend pulled off his black beard and threw it on the ground. He put his hand inside his coat. Then he showed Mr Woodley his gun.

'Yes,' he said. 'I *am* Bob Carruthers.'

'You're too late,' Mr Woodley said. 'She's my wife.'

'And you are dead!' Mr Carruthers said.

A loud noise came from his gun. Mr Woodley fell to the ground and didn't move.

Mr Williamson started to take a gun from his coat, but Holmes was too quick for him.

'Stop!' he said, with his gun in his hand. 'Watson, take his gun. Put it to his head. Thank you. Carruthers, give me your gun, too.'

'Who *are* you?' Mr Carruthers said.

'My name is Sherlock Holmes.' Holmes turned and saw Peter. 'And now we'll send for the police. Peter, take this note to the police station in Farnham,' he said. He wrote a short note. 'Williamson and Carruthers, carry Woodley into the house.'

Some minutes later, Holmes, Mr Williamson and Mr Carruthers were in the sitting room of the house. Miss Smith sat quietly in a bedroom. Mr Woodley was on a bed in one of the other bedrooms. I left him and came down to the sitting room.

'He'll live,' I told them.

'What!' Mr Carruthers shouted. 'Then let's go and kill him! That lovely young woman can't be his wife!'

'She *isn't* his wife,' Holmes said. 'Mr Williamson isn't really a vicar.'

'But –' began Mr Williamson.

'No, you're not!' Holmes said. 'I know about you. You *were* a vicar, but you lost your job.' He turned to Mr Carruthers. 'And you, Carruthers – next time, leave your gun in your coat!'

'I'm sorry, Mr Holmes,' Mr Carruthers said. 'I wanted to help Miss Smith because – because I love her. I always went after her on my bicycle because I wanted to stop these men. She knew my

He put his hand inside his coat.

face, so I wore a beard. I didn't want her to be afraid of me. I didn't want her to leave Chiltern House.'

'But you didn't tell her about Woodley and Williamson, or about the plan,' Holmes said. 'Why?'

'I wanted her to stay at the house with me,' Mr Carruthers answered. 'She didn't love me, but I loved her. Then the note arrived.'

'What note?' Holmes asked.

'A very short note,' Mr Carruthers said. He took it from his coat and read it: *The old man is dead.*'

'So he wasn't dead when you left South Africa,' Holmes said. 'Ah, now I understand.'

'You do?' Mr Carruthers said.

'Yes. The three of you came from South Africa. You, Williamson and Woodley.'

'No!' Mr Williamson said. 'I was never in South Africa. I met the two of them here.'

'That's right,' Mr Carruthers said.

'All right,' Holmes said. 'You and Woodley knew Ralph Smith in South Africa. He said, "After I die, my money will go to Miss Smith." It was a lot of money and you wanted it. So you came to England and looked for her. You had a plan. You wanted her to marry one of you. Then that man had to give half of her money to the other man. Why was Woodley the husband?'

'We played a game of cards,' Mr Carruthers said sadly. 'Woodley won the game.'

'You invited Miss Smith to your house as a music teacher,' Holmes said. 'Woodley wanted her to love him, but she didn't like him. She was afraid of him. And then *you* fell in love with her. You and Woodley had a fight about it. Woodley left and made a new plan.'

'You're right, Mr Holmes,' Mr Carruthers said. 'I heard about Williamson, the vicar, and I began to understand Woodley's new plan. After that, I watched Miss Smith carefully. Then Woodley came to my house with the note from South Africa. Ralph Smith was dead. Woodley said, "I'm going to marry Miss Smith now. Or you can marry her and give me half her money." "I'd like to do that but she doesn't want to marry me," I told him. "Perhaps her feelings will change in a week or two," he said. "I'm not going to hurt her," I told him. And he went away, very angry.

'Miss Smith wanted to leave me, and to go back to London this Saturday. Peter took her to the station in the trap, but I was afraid for her. I went after them on my bicycle. Before I could catch them, Woodley and Williamson took her. Then I saw you in the trap, Mr Holmes. You know the end of the story.'

'I do,' Holmes said. He looked out of the window. 'And here come the police! They'll want to talk to you, Williamson. And to Woodley.' He turned to Carruthers. 'At the beginning, you were as bad as Woodley,' he said. 'But in the end you tried to help Miss Smith. Because you helped her, I will try to help you. I'll talk to the police.'

'Thank you, Mr Holmes,' Mr Carruthers said.

'Watson, go and see Miss Smith,' Holmes said to me. 'We'll take her to her mother. Then we'll send a note to her young man – Cyril. When he arrives, she'll feel better!'

'Yes, Holmes,' I said.

He is usually right.

ACTIVITIES

Sherlock Holmes and the Strange Mr Angel

Before you read

1 Discuss these questions.

   a What do you know about Sherlock Holmes? Where does he live? What does he do? What is the name of his friend and helper?

   b Why do people like reading detective stories?

2 Look at the Word List at the back of the book. Which words are these?

   a You can buy a house here.

   b You can open a lock with this.

   c This person usually works in a house.

   d A horse pulls this.

   e Running shoes have these on the bottom.

While you read

3 Are these sentences right (✓) or wrong (✗)?

   a Mr Windibanks is Miss Sutherland's uncle.   .....

   b Miss Sutherland gives her parents £100 every year.   .....

   c Miss Sutherland met Mr Angel at a dance.   .....

   d Mr Angel wears dark glasses.   .....

   e Miss Sutherland and Mr Angel marry.   .....

   f Mr Windibanks works for a wine company.   .....

   g Mr Angel is a big man with a beard.   .....

   h Miss Sutherland says she will marry another man.   .....

4 What does Sherlock Holmes say? Finish the sentences.

   a 'A man .... an older woman for her money, and for her daughter's ....'

   b 'They didn't want to lose one .... pounds a year when she got married.'

   c 'You didn't think about the .... of a young woman in love.'

   d 'Miss Sutherland will .... for Mr Hosmer Angel.'

40

5 Who says these words? What are they talking about?

    a 'I'm a detective. It's my job.'

    b 'I call him my father.'

    c 'He got *in*. I saw him.'

    d 'Strange things happen, but I'll always love you.'

    e 'We didn't want to hurt her.'

6 Discuss these questions.

    a How does Sherlock Holmes know about Miss Sutherland's job before she tells him?

    b How does Holmes know that Mr Windibanks is Hosmer Angel?

7 Work with another student. Have this conversation.

    Student A: You are Dr Watson. Why didn't Hosmer Angel get out of the cab at the church? How does Holmes know that Mr Windibanks typed the letters to Miss Sutherland. Ask him.

    Student B: You are Sherlock Holmes. Answer Dr Watson's questions.

8 At the end of the story, Watson asks Holmes, 'Will you tell Miss Sutherland all this?' Holmes says no. Is he right? What do you think?

Sherlock Holmes and the Important Exam Paper

Before you read

9 Discuss these questions.

    a Why do students have to do exams? How do you study for them?

    b What happens in this story, do you think? What is the problem with the exam paper? What does Sherlock Holmes have to do?

While you read

10 Which are the right words in each sentence?

    a Holmes goes to the university because he wants to *help somebody/ read some books.*

    b Mr Soames wants the help of *Sherlock Holmes/ the police.*

    c He thinks that somebody *read/ took* an exam paper.

    d Only *Daulat Ras/ Bannister* perhaps knew about the paper before Mr Soames went out.

    e When Mr Soames returned, the visitor hid *under the desk/ in a cupboard.*

    f *Three/ Four* students live in Soames's building.

    g Gilchrist is *good at games/ rich.*

    h Daulat Ras *works/ doesn't work* hard.

    i McLaren *works/ doesn't work* hard.

    j Gilchrist is *tall/ short.*

    k Bannister worked for *McLaren's/ Gilchrist's* father.

After you read

11 Discuss why these are important to Holmes.

    a pieces of a pencil

    b black clay

    c a line and a cut on the top of the desk

    d Bannister's key

    e a tall person

12 What happens to these people at the end of the story?

    a Gilchrist

    b Bannister

13 Did Bannister do anything wrong? What do you think?

14 Work with another student. Have this conversation.

    Student A: You are Watson. How does Holmes know that Gilchrist saw the paper? Ask him questions.

    Student B: You are Holmes. Answer Watson's questions.

Sherlock Holmes and the Dangerous Road

Before you read

15 Talk about these problems

    a A music teacher gets a good job, but it is a long way from her home. What does she do?

    b A man with no money knows a rich girl. How can he get her money?

    c Two men know one rich girl. How can the two of them get her money?

While you read

16 Which answer is right?

    a Who did Miss Smith *not* meet in the London hotel?

        Mr Carruthers   Mr Williamson   Mr Woodley

    b Who is Miss Smith going to marry?

        Ralph Smith   Cyril   Peter

    c Where does Miss Smith teach music?

        at Chiltern House   at Charlington House   in Baker Street

    d Where does Mr Carruthers live?

        near Farnham   in Coventry   in London

    e How does the man follow Miss Smith?

        on a bicycle   in a car   in a horse and trap

    f Where does Dr Watson visit an estate agency?

        in Farnham   in London   in Coventry

    g Who wins Holmes's fight with Mr Woodley?

        Mr Woodley   Holmes   nobody

    h Who does the vicar 'marry' Miss Smith to?

        Cyril   Mr Woodley   Mr Carruthers

    i Who loves Miss Smith?

        Mr Woodley   Mr Williamson   Mr Carruthers

After you read

17 Discuss these questions.

    a Holmes is going to write to Cyril. What will he tell him? What will Cyril do? Will he be angry with Miss Smith? Why (not)?

    b In this story, and in the first story in the book, a young woman has money and people want it. But they have different plans. What are they? Which plan is the cleverest? Which plan is the unkindest?

18 Work with another student. Have this conversation.

    Student A: You are Holmes. Lestrade, a policeman and an old friend, is having tea at your house. Tell him about one of the stories in this book.

    Student B: You are Lestrade. Listen to the story and ask questions. Then ask about Holmes's skills. What can the police learn from him?

Writing

19 A year after Miss Sutherland goes to Sherlock Holmes for help, she sends him a letter. She tells him about her life now. She doesn't know anything about Hosmer Angel. But she is going to marry another man. Write the letter.

20 Write about Mr Windibanks. What is he like? Who is his wife? Why did he not want Miss Sutherland to marry? What did he do?

21 Write a letter from Daurat Ras to his parents in India. In the letter, Ras tells them about Gilchrist and the exam paper.

22 What does Sherlock Holmes do at the university? Write Dr Watson's notes for the story.

23 Write a letter from Gilchrist, now in South Africa, to Holmes. In the letter, Gilchrist thanks Holmes because Holmes didn't tell the university about the exam paper.

24 Write Holmes's note to Cyril at the end of 'Sherlock Holmes and the Dangerous Road'.

25 Which story did you enjoy most? Why?

26 Which other famous detectives do you know from books, films or television? Write about one of them. How are they different from Sherlock Holmes?

WORD LIST *with example sentences*

advertisement (n) I'm looking for a flat. Are there any *advertisements* in today's newspaper?

beard (n) I don't want a *beard*. I don't like hair on a man's face.

cab (n) Let's take a *cab* to the cinema. It's quicker than the bus.

clay (n) This ground is *clay*, so water runs away very slowly.

estate agency (n) Two *estate agencies* are trying to sell my house.

exam (n) After a year of classes, I'll take the English *exam*.

hide (v) *Hide* behind the tree. They can't see you there.

key (n) Can I have the *key* to the front door? I can't get into the house.

kiss (v) He *kissed* his children and said goodbye.

line (n) There's a red *line* across the page. Please don't write anything below that.

lock (v) *Lock* the door to my office. There's a lot of money in my desk.

pencil (n) Have you got a *pencil*? I want to make notes.

piece (n) I'll eat that small *piece* of meat in a sandwich.

secret (n) Nobody at work knows my home telephone number. It's a *secret*.

servant (n) When my parents were rich, they had *servants*. Now my mother does the housework.

spike (n) Be careful with those sports shoes. The *spikes* on the bottom will cut your hand.

trap (n) There were no cars then, but some people had a horse and *trap*.

type (v) Please *type* the letter. Nobody can read your handwriting, and you're a good *typist*.

vicar (n) Who is the *vicar* at that church?

weak (adj) After two weeks in hospital, she felt very *weak*.

The Return of Sherlock Holmes
Sir Arthur Conan Doyle

In 1891, the great detective, Sherlock Holmes, disappeared in Switzerland while working on a dangerous case. Everyone thought that he was dead. But three years later, he returned to England. Holmes and his friend, Dr Watson, had many more adventures together. Three of his most interesting cases are in this book.

A Scandal in Bohemia
Sir Arthur Conan Doyle

All kinds of people, from shopkeepers to kings, want the help of Sherlock Holmes in these six stories about the adventures of the famous detective. Who put a diamond in a chicken? Why is there a club for men with red hair? How did the man at the lake die? Can Sherlock Holmes solve the mysteries?

Sherlock Holmes and the Mystery of Boscombe Pool
Sir Arthur Conan Doyle

Who killed Charles McCarthy? And why? Was it really his son? Sherlock Holmes, the brilliant detective, must answer these questions with the help of this trusted friend, Dr Watson.

The No. 1 Ladies' Detective Agency
Alexander McCall Smith

Precious Ramotswe is a kind, warm hearted and large African lady. She is also the only female private detective in Botswana. Her agency – the No. 1 Ladies' Detective Agency – is the best in the country. With the help of her secretary, Mma Makutsi, and her best friend, Mr JLB Matekoni, she solves a number of difficult – and sometimes dangerous – problems. A missing husband, a missing finger and a missing child – she will solve these mysteries in her own special way.

K's First Case
L.G. Alexander

This is a detective story with a difference. We invite *you* to help solve the case.

Katrina Kirby is a detective, and people call her 'K'. There has been a murder in a big country house. K knows that one of five people murdered Sir Michael Gray. Who did it? How? Why?

The Ring
Bernard Smith

One day Rafael was well; the next day he was completely mad. What happened to make him crazy? The story of Rafael and his gold ring is a story of murder, mystery and love. Many people know part of the story, but only Rafael knows what really happened. And Rafael is mad.

There are hundreds of Penguin Readers to choose from – world classics, film adaptations, modern-day crime and adventure, short stories, biographies, American classics, non-fiction, plays ...

For a complete list of all Penguin Readers titles, please contact your local Pearson Longman office or visit our website.

www.penguinreaders.com

Longman Dictionaries

Express yourself with confidence!

Longman has led the way in ELT dictionaries since 1935. We constantly talk to students and teachers around the world to find out what they need from a learner's dictionary.

Why choose a Longman dictionary?

Easy to understand

Longman invented the Defining Vocabulary – 2000 of the most common words which are used to write the definitions in our dictionaries. So Longman definitions are always clear and easy to understand.

Real, natural English

All Longman dictionaries contain natural examples taken from real-life that help explain the meaning of a word and show you how to use it in context.

Avoid common mistakes

Longman dictionaries are written specially for learners, and we make sure that you get all the help you need to avoid common mistakes. We analyse typical learners' mistakes and include notes on how to avoid them.

Innovative CD-ROMs

Longman are leaders in dictionary CD-ROM innovation. Did you know that a dictionary CD-ROM includes features to help improve your pronunciation, help you practice for exams and improve your writing skills?

For details of all Longman dictionaries, and to choose the one that's right for you, visit our website:

www.longman.com/dictionaries